TERE 3 YA MERE 3

THREE SKITS

ARVIND R. KURIL

Made with ♥ on the Notion Press Platform
www.notionpress.com

Devoted to all my learners who are in search of knowledge in dramatic way.

ARVIND

Contents

Foreword

So what do you want to be in your life?

You only have to think and decide.

Why to ask someone.

Enjoy the play.

Keep learning.

Arvind

Preface

I am happy to share with you the skits which was written and execute among many of my learning communities.

This is the raw scrip for the same.

If you want to replicate and do it, you are always welcome.

Do let me know if you need any assistance.

magicarvind@gmail.com

Arvind

Acknowledgements

I take this opportunity to thank all my near dear ones who always wanted me to happy, jolly, sharing and open to listen.

I also like to thank all my colleagues who contributed with love and affection. Without them it was little difficult to execute.

Thank you for you, because you are the ultimate appreciator reader.

Hope you will get an immense pleasure and joy after finishing this book.

It has 3 classic roleplay/skit/drama ever created by me.

Keep learning.

Arvind R. Kuril

Prologue

The book contains 3 dramas/skits/roleplay included.

It will make you laugh at some point of time and sometimes a sattire so that you will think about the situation.

All 3 deliveries are in raw state.

So do make changes if you want to execute.

Hope to see you reading and learning.

Arvind

CHAPTER ONE

ROCHAK

Participants :

Aarefa Soni : Aarefa

Maahit Doshi : Doctor/NGO

Jash Sanghvi : Instagram

Yuv Jain : Dad / Whatsapp

Maahir Jain : Facebook

Duration of Skit = 5 mins max

Name of Skit : "Social Media se janme maansik tanaav se mukti"

****

SCENE-1

(Three people comes in front of the stage by wearing back labadda....mentioned like facebook, instagram and whatsapp)

Facebook : aakhir aa gayee app, aap sabkaa swagat hai, yahaan....main facebook aur mere saathi... insta aur whatsaap milkar aapke vichaaron ka kachoomar nikaalenge.

Instagram : Haan, chalo in sabke saath saath, shuruwaat karte hain.

Whatsapp : Wo dekho! Wo ladki abhi tak sirf phone ka hi upyog kar rahee hai..chalo usey whatsapp/fb aur insta ki latt lagaayen....

SCENE-2

(On stage dad and her daughter... Aarefa started using phone, then dad makes her)

Dad : Arefa, kyaa baat hai betaa, mom bata rahee thee, online class khatam hone ke baad bhi tum phone me lagi rahtee ho?

Aarefa : nahi pappa, wo assignment kar rahee thee isliye phone rakhnaa padtaa hai.

Dad ; mammi ne batayaa, school mein bhi tum phone chup chup kar upyog me la rahee ho.... Teacher ne complain kiya hai..

Aarefa: wo wo... pappa! Haamare doston ka ek whatsapp group banaa hai, usme ham chat karte rahte hain...

Dad: kya chat? Bachchon ko toh aapas mein baat karnee chahiye. Chat se kiska pet bhartaa hai. Dekho... ye sab ab band karo aur padhaayee par dhyaan do..

Aarefa. : theek hai papa.

(she stops for a while and continues to chat on phone....enjoys and time passes)

Dad: (shouts) ye kyaa abhi bhi chatting. Manaa kiyaa thaa na... fir se chatting....mom sahee bolti thee iss ladki ko toh din bhar chatting...chatting aur chatting hi chahiye.... (scolds) kitne dino se ye sab chal rahaa hai? haan!

Aarefa : na dad.. Just a min.... Ek smilyee bhejti hoon fir bataati hoon... (stops and talks)

Papa: wo ye jab se aapne phone diyaa hai tab se...!

Aarefa : papa,, aapko nahi pataa, ye whatsapp/facebook aur insta se ham kabhi bhee kaheen bhi kisi se bhi baat kar saktey hain... ye mobile nahi duniyaa ki khidki hai...papa bass.. Ab aap jao .. mere online friends meraa wait kar rahe honge... mammi

ko main samjha doongi!

(she continues chatting and .... Walks away)

Dad : kyaa jamaana hai, bachpan mein maa ki suno, fir patni ki aur ab bachho kee...kisi ko samjhaana ek tedhee kheer ban gayee hai! (walks away)

SCENE-3

(aarefa keeps chatting....suddenly found her account got hacked...)

Aarefa : Oh MY God!, meri social media ka login aur password kisi ne hack kar lee...ab meri image ka kyaa hoga..kaun ho sktaa hai?

(FB along with Instaa and Whatsapp... enters)

Instaa : haa haa, haa,,, ab tum hamaara shikaar ho....

FB : Ab ham tumhaari saari details leke, usey badalkar ... duniyaa me failaa denge... tumhe badnaam kar denge

Insta : aur tumhaare pass samay hi nahee hoga isey sudhaarne, ka....

FB: tumhaara jeevan ab hamaare kadmo me hai.... Ha ha haa...ab tumhaari jindagi ki ghadiyaan khatm samjho.. aur haan ye jo ho rahaa hai, uski jimmedar tum khud ho,....tumne apnaa jeevan barbaad kar diya...bekaar ki chatting mein...browsing mein...ab bhugto....

(all three....makes action towards aarefa and she screams and faints down, dad comes and calls the doctor)

Doctor : isey thoda bukhaar hai par lagtaa hai ye stress (TANAAV) mein hai, kisi baat ne isey bahut pareshaan kar rakha hai...

Dad : haa ye hameshaa phone par bani rahtee thee. Chatting se door hee nahi rahtee.

Doctor : Offoh!!, fir toh ye kaafi gambheer samsya hai. Yahi samasya to saare duniyaa ko lag chuki hai.

Doctor:(writes something on notepad/ medicine prescription and says...)

Main aarefa ke liye thodi medicines likh detaa hoon. Main ek NGO - Maansik Swasthya Sangathan ka sadasya bhi hoon. Aarefa ke liye kuch sessions karwaa deta hoon,, jisase ye samajh jayegi...ki kaise apne aap ko inn sab samasyaaon se door rakhaa jaaye...

SCENE-4

(doctor along with members in NGO)

NGO/Doctor : (to dad) dekhiye, ghabraane ki aavashyaktaa nahi hai, Chatting ki aadat aur social media ke kaaran bahut se bachcho me ye samasyaa hone lagti hai. Lekin isasey bachney ka badaa aasan tareeka hai....

Dad : wo kya?

NGO/Doctor :(facing towards audience)

sabse pahle, bachchon ko seemit samay ke liye hi phone dein,

bachchon se unke doston ke baare mein jaankari lein.

Samay samay par paarivar ka mahattva darshane ke liye apnepan ka ahsaas hona aavashyak hai..

aapko apne bachchon ko dishaa nirdesh dekar unko samjhaana hoga ki in sabki kitni aavashyaktaa hai

(tabhi aarefa ko hosh aataa hai aur wo poochti hai)

Aarefa : aur mere account jo hack ho gaya hai uska kyaa hoga? Uncle ?

NGO/Doctor : uski chinta na karo, betaa! cyber cell kee sahaayata se hackers ko pakad liye jaayega, likin tumhe bhi dhyaan rakhna hai kee, social media par har kisi sebaat karnaa khatre se bharaa hai.

DAD : (facing towards audience)

Pyaare bachchon aur saathiyon!

Aur kisi bhi aisi ghatnaa ko apne parivaar se avashyaa bataayein, taaki ham aap sabhi bachcho ki jald se jald sahaayata kar sakein.

NGO/Doctor:

Ant mein, kisi bhi aisi sansthaa jo logon ke bhalayee ke liye kaam karti ho, unse sahayaata lene mein der na karein... jaise hamaari sansthaa...

"Maansik Swasthya Sangathan!!"

(all bows down)

****

CHAPTER TWO

National Integration

News Anchor with Gajra (+ Narrator) News-Anchor Formal

Manoj Kumar (actor) Khaadi / Indian outfit

Goongi (dumb) Simple - but old clothes

Langdi (one legged) Simple - but old clothes

Looli (hand broken) Simple - torn clothes

Andhee (blind) Simple - old saree/salwar

Bahree (deaf) Simple - old saree/salwar

Bhoodhee (very old lady) White hair wig, white cloth

New Bharat Maata Attire of Mother India

- Dhol / Tablas - Songs

Also song runs - Hum logo ko samajh sako to...(song ends)

Everyone sings and claps with the song - Dhundho Dhundo re bharat, dhoondo re bhaarat, kahaan gaya mera bhaarat.

(enters the news anchor)

Anchor : Mera gajra lagao re koi, main to bhaarat khojne jaa rahee hoon. Interview loongi uskaa. Pata nahee kab se gaayab hai. Mil nahee rahaa. Bhaarat O bhaarat. Arey bhaarat maata bhi mil jaati toh achchaa thaa.

(background song- mere desh ki dhartee sona ugale.... stops)

Manoj : Hey, main hoon bharat, main hoon bhaarat kumar. Maine kitnee saari filmein banayee bharat par, deshbhakti par, aur a sab mujhe bharat kumaar ke naam se bhi pukaaratey hai. Sun lo ye saboot hai ...

Anchor : arey ye to actor hai, achcha baitho thodi der. mujhe sureeli bhaarat maata chahiye.

(background song - ??... stops)

Goongi : Abba dabba chabba

Anchor : kyaa chahiye

Goongi : Abba dabba chabba, speaks like - aa, aee, oooae (showing expression that she is the one)

Anchor : chup kar, uss kone main baith jaa, mujhe chamakdaar bhaarat maata chahiye.

Anchor : baat to sach hai, achcha tum baitho thodi der. mujhe sach much ki bhaarat maata chahiye.

(background song - ??... stops)

Loolee : aga mee ikdey aahe, kaahee dya ani kaay pan karaa, Anchor : matlaalab kya re baba

Loolee : matlab KAYDAA, kahee dya re baba, 2 paise 5 paise

Anchor : aise kaise paise mang ree re

Loolee : paise manjhe rupayee, sab bhikhaari hain, loan de re baba, ghar de re baba, bachchaa de re baba, sona de re babam kursee de rebaba, isliye maieech looli bharat maata. Aati kaayde anusaar kaahi dyaa!

Anchor : ok, ok, you take, note fake, baitho wait karo, mujhe chamakdaar bhaarat maata chahiye.

(background song - yeh andhaa kanoon hai... stops)

Andhee : ye kyaa ho rahaa hai, ye kyaa ho rahaa hai, dekho mujhe dikhaao main kaise dikh rahee hoon. Dekho, dekho, mai bhaarat maata hoon, main dekh nahee saktee jaise apnaa kanoon nahee dekh saktaa, taareekh-pe-tareekh hee dikhtee hai, jaise road ke khadde muncipality ko nahee dikhtaa, bheekh maangtey bachche logo ko nahee dikhtey, jhopadee mein rahne waale gareeb log ammeron ko nahee dikhtey, rape case par sajaa ka kanoon ban gaya par logo ko abhi bhi bachchee aur betiyaa nahee dikhtee.

Main hee hoon bharat maata in logo kee.

Anchor : sachchee re sab andhey hain, lekin mujhe maloom bharat maata aise nahee nahee aur bhee achchee hai, tum bhi baitho main aage dekhtee hoon. Aiee baayee jara bajoo hat, khojney de bharat maata ko

(background song - ??... stops)

(Entrees with earphones/headphones)

Bahree : kyaa boli

Anchor : main bhaarat khoj rahee hoon,

Bahree : kyaa boli, khairaat bhej rahee hoon, to mujhe hi de do, jaroorat hai, kyonki mai hee bharat hoon. Mujhe sab sunaayee deta hai, jaise election mein phopooo sunayee deta hai, baad mein achche din aayenge sunaayee detaa hai, fir demonetization sunayee detaa hai fir avishwaas prastaav sunaayee detaa hai, pappu aur feku sunaayee detaa hai... main hee hoon bhaarat maata

Anchor : nayee re baaba, apnee bharat maata aisee toh nahee thee,

(background song - ??... stops)

Boodhee : sahee bolaa betee, ab keval main hee ban saktee hoon bharat maata, dekho himalaya ke barf jaise meri choteee, bahtee nahdiyon jaisey mere khoon ke daag, har jagah jale huye makaanon jaisa meraa shareer, main hee hoon bharat maata.

Anchor : Oh! Big problem, agar tum sab logo jaisee problems bharat mein hai to kaun hai jo mere pyaare bharat ko sahee roop mein banaayega? Kau hai jo hamaare kho gaye bharat ko nayaa roop degaa?

ALL : ye sab log!

Anchor : Haan sahee hai, ye naujawan peedhee hee hai jo apnee achchey vichaaron se nayee bharat ko banaa sakte hai. Yahee hain jo bharat maata ka svachch sundar roop de saktaa hai.

Toh aao ham sab milkar ek nayee bhaarat ko banayein jisame sabhi ek doosarey ka aadar kar sakein, sabhi ko surakhsaa miley aur sabhee ko behatar jindagee aur aagey badhney ka haq.

(new bharat maata enters from back stage)

ALL : Jai Hind , Jai Bharat!

(song runs - with a happiness among all - India waale...)

CHAPTER THREE

Yo Se Mera Haryana

Characters : 3 friends meeting for a small chat

Friend (1) : Dahiya : Neevan

Dahiya's Wife : Mitthu : Amatullah

Friend (2) : Kundu : Nemin

Friend (3) : Punia : Vihaan

BEGINS...

Video Link: Yo Se Mera Haryana

(22) यो सै मेरा हरियाणा - Yo Se Mera Haryana - Ajay Soda - New Haryanvi Cultural Song - Singham Haryanvi - YouTube

Students will move and dance on the stage with a specific step related to HARYAANA

Scene-1

Dahiya is sitting with a grumpy face on a desk and dangling his legs.

Punia sees him from his window and approaches him

Punia : K chal rahya se ? (whats going on)

Dahiya just nods his head to and fro and does'nt answer

Punia : k chakker hai ? (whats the problem?)

Dahiya : Mitthu !

Punia : Mittu ? voh toh tarhi birrni (gharali) hai, kya bolri hai

Kundu: namaskar dostoh! Kis vishay par charcha ho rahi hai?

Punia: yeh agayo hamaro (delhi) shudh hindi boli walo bawlo

Dhaniya laughs

Dhahiya : chora ki hazri jawabee!

Punia : tu tari khabar bata! Yeh muh kyu latkaya hai tara, thare chehre pe 12 baje gaye dikkh re sey

Dhaiya : toh baat yeh hai ki : hamari shrimati koh jana hai london reheneh hamesha , hamesha keh liyeh. Leking Mujhe mera haryana hai pyaara, aur idhar meri bir, meri ardhangini, meri mitthu, mujhse ehsi mangein karke rula rahi hai, ab toh naak me dam kar diyaa hai..

Punia : Dahiya, baat toh saanchi ye, pann aadhmi thodi laaz - saram toh rakhey hey, zindagi mein itna sakth bano keh pyaaz (kaanda) keh siva koi bhi rula na sakeh, thaari lugai baabli ho gayee se.

Kundu : Mitr Punia! aap toh dahiya keh jeevan mein dahi ka rayta jyaada hi fayla rahe hai. Idhar ujjwal bahvishya keh liyeh bhabhiji karna chahati hai namasteh London aur aap Puniaji kyo YO mera Haryana bol rahe ho...

Punia : Haan yaarron, kadardaano, mere pyaareh dostoh!

Aayeh desi rap suniyeh ! aur samjeh harayana keh goon, gyan, gaurav!

Kundu : dil tham keh baithe! Dahiya ji, kripa kar keh leh aayeeyeh aapki srimati koh! Zara

voh bhi toh suniyeh hamari haryana kee laajawaab baatein

Video Link: ????

Yo Haryana Hai Pardhan (Lyrics)

(22) Yo Haryana Hai Pardhan (Lyrics) - KD | Raju Punjabi | New Haryanvi Song 2020 | Lyrics Of Vikey - YouTube

(Dahiya drags his wife and gets her there and says.......

https://www.youtube.com/watch?v=gPcS3tX-XiI

KARAOKE

Kundu : Dekho bhabhi , Londan mein hai, bhaavnaaon ka अभाव , सेंट्रल लंदन - एक aisee जगह है, jahaan samasyaayein adhik hain, काम की प्रकृति bdalati rahtee hai, tola-maasha-ratti ke log apna zameer bech dete hai,पर्यावरण संबंधी चिंताएं और स्थिरता lagataar

badhati hee ja rahee hai.

Dahiya sings : Aaja ajaa, birni, ... Yoh seh mera haryana (first few lines)

(Dahiya , Punia, Kundu all together sing : desi mitro! Chaliyeh Rap kareh

Video Link:

Punia :

javaanoh ki dharti kisaanoh ki dharti

dangal akhaade pahalwanoh ki dharti

Dharti maata peh maatha laga kar pravesh kareh

mera haryana bhagwano ki dharti

Kundu :

aa jao jee aap ka swaagat hai man se

feel mat kariyo jee thode bahot fun se

Foolmala wala to riwaaz hai puraana jee

entry karayenge kya gabbar keh gun se

Dahiya :

dariyo na bhabhi shahab log saare achhe hai,

kaaleja clean hai, thode akal ke kachche hai

maan seh toh hum sareh bachche hai

(song stops)

Mithu :

Waa waa waa! RAP toh achchaa thaa!

... lekin itnaa bolne se hi Haryaana mein koi kyon rukega?

Koi proof hai kya jisasey pataa chale ki yahaa rukne ke baad sachmuch logo ka jeevan badal jaata hai.

Sirf gine chune log hi, oopar uthh paate honge.

Dahiya : Haa..haann... un gine chuno mein zaraa naam toh suno.....

Juhi Chawla, brahmand Sundari hai hamareh Ambala ke gaon ki

Haryana keh toofani ballebaj kapil Dev ji layeh vishwa cup desh ke liye

Faridabaad ke sonu nigam ji ki sureeli aawaj mann koh behalaaye

Ramdev baba keh patanjali batayeh ayurveda keh gunnn

Hisar gaon keh Jindal ji vishva keh steel keh vyapari

Kundu :

Bhiwani keh Kejri walji aaj baneh delhi keh CM ji

Virendra Shewag neh maree thignee century cricket mein

Virendra singh Ji neh Olympics aur asian boxing mein kiya desh ka naam Roshan

ZEE MEDIA aur Essel world ke malik Subhash Chandra Goenka aur

India bulls company keh malik Sameer Gehlaut bhi harayana seh

Neeraj Chopra layeh gold hamare desh ke liye javelin throw mein

Sania nehwal keh badminton mein kiya desh ka naam roshan

Punia : Arrey bhojan bhaatt toh rah hi gayaa,

Haryana ke pakwan sabse lazeydar :

Razma chawal ;

aloo bajra ki roti,

dahi vada ya ho kadhi pakoda!

Haryana hai swadisht bhojan bhaatt aur khana ka khazana.

Dahiya : HAMAARI SHAADI ki mithaiyaan, Mithe pakvaan, meri mittu, bhoolya gee k!

Besan keh ladoo; meethe pudhe; rabadi aur M M mithaiwala ka aloo ka halwa

Meri mittu jasia madhur sukhad swadhith nirala.

Maan.jaaa meri mittu rani , saareh jahan seh acha hindustan mera!

Mera haryana bhagwan ki dharti

Meri mittu laya tere liyeh mein 52 gaj ka daman

London nahi haryana mein hai sara bhramand racha...

Mittu : dahiya teri baat mein to hai ab maine maani, abb main London naa jaani

Haryaana ki mitti ab toh lagne laagi paavan

Ab mangwaao mere liye 52 gaj ka daaman

Dahiyaa: Kee baat sey, baat ban gayee..

Punia : Oye baabdi ab samajhdaar ho gayee sey!! Dahiyaaa....Dilwaa de abb 52 gajj...inhe

(song plays and everyone dances)

Video Link: 0.35 to 1:17

(22) 52 GAJ KA DAMAN | PRANJAL DAHIYA | AMAN JAJI | RENUKA PANWAR | MUKESH JAJI | SAHIL SANDHU - YouTube

The End

https://www.youtube.com/watch?v=DaJsa97AUsw

Leave A Feedback

Hope you had enjoyed the dra/skit/role play.

Drop me your feedback/reflections on this.

magicarvind@gmail.com

See you soon with a new arrival soon.

Keep Learning

Arvind

9 798889 754633

Printed by Libri Plureos GmbH in Hamburg, Germany